THE GREEKS IN AMERICA

The IN AMERICA *Series*

THE **GREEKS** IN AMERICA

JAYNE CLARK JONES

Published by
Lerner Publications Company
Minneapolis, Minnesota

...CONTENTS...

Temple of Olympian Zeus, Athens. The Olympic Games, held every four years, were the greatest festival in ancient Greece. The first of the modern Olympics was held in Athens in 1896. Since that time, they have been held in major cities throughout the world.

Introduction

For America, Greece can never be just another hungry Balkan country. Our public buildings and great institutions are still being built to resemble ancient Greek temples. Our dictionaries are full of Greek words. Our museums contain Greek pottery and sculpture. Even beginning students of philosophy know about Plato and Aristotle. Those who study poetry learn about Homer, Pindar, and Sappho. Every year in American theatres and films it is possible to see a play by Aeschylus, Sophocles, or Euripides. There are as many pictures of the Parthenon in our papers and magazines as there are of the Golden Gate Bridge or the White House. Ladies wear gowns which leave one shoulder uncovered and they are called "Grecian" gowns.

Of all the things we have borrowed from ancient Greek civilization, the one we value more than any other is the form of government chosen by Thomas Jefferson and the founders of our country. We prize it so highly that we have tried to teach it to the whole world. We still call it by its Greek name: Democracy. For these reasons America has always been especially interested in the affairs of Greece.

The Greeks call themselves *Hellenes;* their country, *Hellas.* Sometimes the term *Hellas* refers to all traditionally Greek lands. *Panhellenic* means "all the Greeks." A *Philhellene* is someone who loves Greece. To *Hellenize* something means to make it more Greek.

PART I

Greek Emigration through the Nineteenth Century

1. *Colonization in Classical Times: The First Greek Emigrants*

The real reason for Greek emigration is to be found in the geography of Greece itself. Mainland Greece is a small peninsular country with an enormously long, irregular coastline. The land that can be cultivated is divided into fairly small parcels by very high, rugged mountains. The mountains and the sea give Greece her special beauty and determine her way of life. Roads through the mountains have always been few and dangerous so that people have traveled over them as little as possible. For this reason, the inland areas of Greece have always been isolated from each other.

Construction of a mask for a modern production of the Greek drama, *House of Atreus*. Masks were originally used in ancient Greek drama to represent the character portrayed by the actor. A different mask was made for each emotion to be expressed.

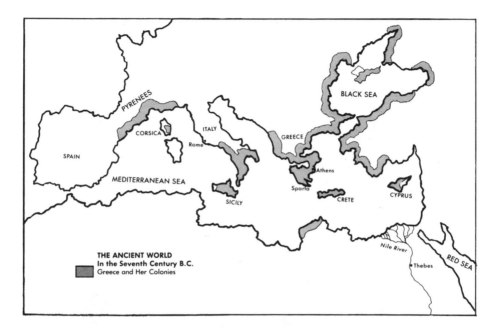

THE ANCIENT WORLD
In the Seventh Century B.C.
Greece and Her Colonies

But no one is very far from the main highway of Greece, the sea. With agricultural land scarce and poor, Greece has faced the same problem again and again: too many people for the resources of the land. The sea provides a way out for the Greeks. Those with too little can sail away. Others can bring back food and goods for those who remain.

Long before classical times (500–400 B.C.) the people of Greece had organized their society around what we now call city-states. The largest town or city of a region was inhabited by the people who owned and cultivated the surrounding land. In this town the government, politics, and civilized life of the area were concentrated. But the populations of these little states soon outgrew the ability of the land to support them. Too many people with too little to eat will, sooner or later, disrupt the order of any society. As early as the eighth century B.C. the city-states of ancient Greece had begun to solve their problems of political discontent and over-population by sending out their citizens as colonists.

The emigrants were bound to the mother city by ties of loyalty, affection, and commerce, but they were free to seek their fortunes and govern themselves in a new land. Traditionally they took with them the blessings of their fellow citizens and fire from the sacred hearth of the mother city with which to kindle a new hearth.

They went everywhere the sea would take them, settling and trading: Sicily, southern Italy and France, along the shores of Asia Minor, the Black Sea, Africa, and all the islands in between. They carried their language and culture with them, sometimes Hellenizing their neighbors but always retaining their character as Greeks.

Greek vase, sixth century B.C., *Hercules Wrestling the Cretan Bull*. The Greek vases are among the finest examples of ancient art. Many of them are in American collections.

The Parthenon was built on the Acropolis at Athens 2,500 years ago. The sculptures of the Parthenon are considered to be among the world's greatest works of art.

By 450 B.C., because of their colonies and trade, the Greek city-states dominated the Mediterranean world. The greatest of them all was Athens. Here, for the first time in history, a great power was governed by democratic means. The mighty Athenian navy was able to regulate trade on the Mediterranean and demand tribute from subject states. As the center of the cultural world, Athens attracted artists, philosophers, scientists, and writers, as well as their students. Athens was a proud city; her citizens were proud of her. She was enriched and beautified by the creations of her sculptors, architects, and metalworkers. She was glorified by dramatists, poets, and orators. In everything from her pottery to her temples, Athens set the standards of style and beauty. During the fifth century B.C., the Parthenon was built on the Athenian acropolis. It was then, and has been ever since, a symbol of the best things attained by Greek civilization. Our own civilization rests on foundations laid in Athens 25 centuries ago.

However, it was not so easy to be a world power, and for Athens, there was too much to learn and too little time to learn it. Old rivals led by Sparta began a war which lasted for nearly 30 years. After years of see-saw battling, at a time when a firm and united government might have saved Athens, her leaders took up political habits so old that they may be national characteristics. They quarreled among themselves and disagreed about what action to take. Their uncertain policy was fatal. When Athens finally surrendered in 404 B.C., her navy had been destroyed and her empire broken up. Without them, her power was gone forever.

But, as so often happens, the winners lost too. The long ruinous war had also weakened the other great city-states. Although groups of city-states had once united in leagues for protection and trade, and managed to keep peace for certain panhellenic athletic contests and religious festivals, they were never able to achieve the panhellenic union which might have saved them. Eventually a new power presided over the movements of the Greek-speaking people.

2. *Alexander and a New Era of Greek Emigration*

To the north of Greece lay the independent kingdom of Macedonia. Though the Greeks of the city-states considered the Macedonians barbarians, under their powerful and clever king, Philip II (382–336 B.C.), Macedonia was able to control the city-states of Greece. Philip spoke Greek and had a Greek education, and he knew how to take advantage of the quarreling Greeks. He kept them weak by encouraging and even provoking disputes among them. When Philip was assassinated at an early age, his young son Alexander inherited his father's army and his problems. The army was a very good one composed of Macedonians and mercenary Greek soldiers. Rather than waste it in the hopeless task of trying to subdue all the Greeks who continued to scheme and plot against him, Alexander set out for the coast of Asia Minor where he planned to free Greek lands and people from Persian rule. The Greeks, then as always, responded to the cause of Greek independence. A good many of them stopped fighting and followed Alexander in his campaign against the Persians. He was so phenomenally successful that he became known as Alexander the Great. He marched through country after country in the east: Syria, Palestine, Egypt, Babylon, Persia, all the way to India. Finally his army, tired of years of campaigning, threatened mutiny and Alexander turned back. He died of a fever at the age of 33 (323 B.C.) in Babylon. He had no time to organize his vast empire, but his armies left the mark of Greece throughout the east. Alexander rewarded his soldiers with gifts of land in the conquered territory if they would make their homes there and garrison the new lands. Many veterans took advantage of this.

Alexander the Great (356-323 B.C.) pushed the boundaries of the Greek empire to their farthest geographical extent. He liberated Greek lands and people from Persian rule, and carried Greek culture throughout the known world.

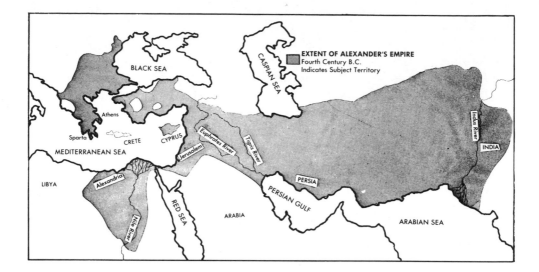

After Alexander died his lands were divided among several of his generals. They encouraged colonists to come and strengthen the new Greek cities in the east. The city-states of Greece were again overpopulated. So were many Greek cities in Asia Minor, some of which had themselves begun as colonies from the mainland. Greek settlers left them to go farther east to the new frontiers or to settle in Egypt. They carried and spread their language and culture as they went.

Alexander's successors and the families (dynasties) they founded ruled for nearly 200 years. By the time they began to weaken and fall, the people of the distant, isolated eastern Greek cities were no longer Greek. They had become part of the native population. But the new cities (such as Alexandria and Antioch) and many old ones in Egypt, Syria, and other lands near the sea or on trade routes had become truly Greek. The ruling class, merchants, artists, craftsmen, and professional people were all Greek. The native people remained only as peasants or shepherds in the lowest classes of society. Common Greek or *koine* was the language of commerce and civilization. In art, science, philosophy, and literature the "Hellenistic" Greeks of the east made great contributions to Greek culture. This Greek world was the one into which the new power of Rome began to expand in the second century before Christ.

3. *The Eastern Roman Empire (Byzantium)*

The city-states of mainland Greece resented the manipulation by Macedonian kings which continued through 200 B.C. When the Greeks invited the Romans to be their ally against Philip V, they were thinking only of being free of Macedonian meddling. The Romans promised to protect Greek freedom and independence, but they began a rule in Greece that was more harsh and rigid than any that had gone before. Then the Roman wave began to surge over the east, swallowing one country after another — nothing could withstand it for long. After conquest came organization into the imperial system. In western Europe when the tribal people of the French and German forests were conquered, they had everything to learn from the Romans: city life, political organization, social system, and even language. They "Romanized" the west. The Hellenized east was another thing altogether.

Hippocrates (460-370 B.C.), the father of modern medicine, brought logic and reason to the practice of medicine. The Hippocratic Oath named after him gave the medical profession a code which emphasized its duty to mankind.

The Romans were always in awe of Greek culture. Greek traders had been selling their beautiful things to the tribes of Italy when Rome was just a country town. Well-educated Romans knew both languages and were well acquainted with Greek literature. They often chose Greek slaves to tutor their children; they sent their older sons to Athens, Rhodes, Pergamum, and Alexandria for their "university" education in oratory, philosophy, medicine, and science. In the complex, sophisticated city life of the east, Roman rule changed very little. But the empire was too big to handle. Enemies within and enemies without kept Rome at war year after year. When Roman power began to give way to repeated barbarian attacks from all sides, the Hellenized eastern part of the Roman Empire proved to be the most stable.

In 395 A.D. the Roman Empire was divided into two parts with Rome the capital of the western half and Constantinople capital of the eastern. The Roman Empire of the east is the Byzantine Empire whose emperors considered themselves Roman but whose language, culture, officials, and citizens were Greek.

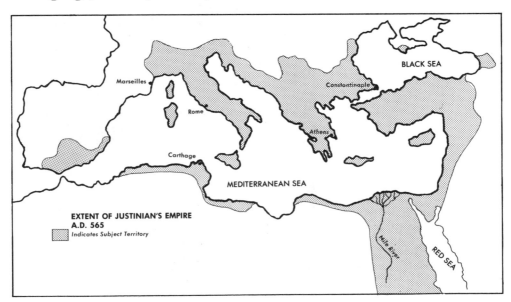

EXTENT OF JUSTINIAN'S EMPIRE
A.D. 565
Indicates Subject Territory

The Byzantine Empire marks the greatest extent of Greek power in history. It rested firmly on an ancient foundation of a flourishing economy and a highly developed city life. The Byzantine Greeks, with the aid and encouragement of their government, became the traders of the Mediterranean world. The Byzantine navy protected commerce on the high seas. Constantinople itself formed the hub of trade routes which linked the Far East and the West. Because of their wealth, powerful cities, and secure government, the Byzantines were able to survive many of the same pressures which forced the collapse of the Roman Empire in the west.

Also, under the Byzantine Emperors, Christianity was officially recognized and supported. Eventually church officials were allowed to control a great deal of property and to exercise certain civil powers as well. The Emperors lent their power and protection to what became the Eastern Orthodox Church.

But Byzantium did not survive as one huge empire from beginning to end. Byzantium and Rome quarreled and fought over territorial and religious matters. In the north they were plagued by barbarian invasions from century to century: Slavs and Avars came from the north, Persians from the east. Finally, after the death of Mohammed in 632 A.D., the Islamic peoples began the attacks which ended in the complete destruction of the Byzantine Empire. The Arabs began, in the seventh century, whittling away the eastern provinces of Syria, Palestine, Egypt, and North Africa. The Ottoman Turks ended it all in 1453 when they captured Constantinople.

4. *Greek Emigration under the Ottomans*

The Ottoman Turks, a small minority in their conquered territory, did not have the manpower or experience to govern their unwieldy empire. Although the Turkish Sultans were absolute monarchs, the early ones were capable rulers. They wisely chose to use the talents and skills of conquered people for their own purposes. The Greeks, with their traditions of education and civil service, were ready to be used. They played a large part in the administration of the Turkish Empire. Greek subjects in other walks of life were allowed to go on very much as before. Farmers, fishermen, sailors, and merchants were unmolested. Some Jews and Orthodox Christians who had been persecuted under western governments were even relieved by the Turkish policy of religious toleration.

In 1453 when Constantinople fell to the Turks, the nations of western Europe were on the verge of their great age of discovery, exploration, and colonization. But the fortunes of all the conquered peoples were tied to Turkish interests. Since the Turks now controlled the trade routes from the east, they needed no Northwest Passage. Their ambition was to expand into Europe, and therefore, they were not interested in claiming new lands across the seas.

A Greek sailor named John is said to have been among the crewmen with Christopher Columbus when he reached the New World.

However, Greek-speaking people were, as much as ever, a part of the maritime world which was becoming so lively just then. Very early in the records of the Spanish expeditions to the New World the names of Greek sailors, pilots, captains, and merchants can be found.

Perhaps, if there had been no Ottoman Empire, the old Greek Empire might have become a modern maritime nation with its capital in Constantinople rather than in Athens and an altogether different history of discovery and exploration might have unfolded. As it was, for nearly 400 years, Hellas was only a memory in the minds of Greek-speaking Turkish citizens.

5. *Earliest Greeks in America*

In 1527, the King of Spain gave to a Spanish nobleman, Narváez, a grant to all the Florida lands previously discovered by Ponce de Leon and Juan de Garay. The story of Narváez's travels, which lasted until 1537, tells of the exploits of a Greek sailor named Theodore who was with him. After a storm caused serious damage to the ships, he helped repair them with pine resin. When the expedition was in the neighborhood of Pensacola (Florida) and in desperate need of fresh water, they arranged to have it brought out to the ships on rafts by the local Indians. Theodore insisted on going ashore with the Indians and though they returned, Theodore never did. In 1540, when DeSoto's expedition was passing through Alabama, the Indians told him about a Christian who had been there from the time of Narváez. They also produced a dagger which they said had been his and told DeSoto that he had been killed. Theodore was the first Greek we know to have set foot on American soil.

A number of Greeks are listed in the chronicles of various Spanish explorers in the New World. A Greek sailor named John sailed with Columbus, and it is said that he believed Cuba to be part of the mainland because he could not imagine such a large island. Magellan had three Greeks with him when he went through the straits at the tip of South America, later called the Straits of Magellan. Moreover, when Sir Francis Drake, in 1578, and Thomas Cavendish, in 1588, first arrived on the west coast of South America, they were able to hire Greek pilots who were thoroughly familiar with the waters off Chile and Peru.

During these years the sea rivalry between the Spanish and the English was very fierce. When Drake and Cavendish appeared on the west coast of New Spain the Spanish believed that these Englishmen had somehow found the Northwest Passage. Of course, the English had sailed around South America just as everyone else did but their presence in the Pacific unnerved the Spaniards. They were determined to find and blockade the western outlet of the supposed Northwest Passage which they called the Straits of Anian.

The Viceroy of Mexico organized an expedition of three ships and 100 men and entrusted them to a Greek seaman whom they called Juan de Fuca. De Fuca had been employed by the Spanish for 40 years. He had been in the West Indies, California, and the Philippines. He had even been robbed of his personal fortune when the English privateer Thomas Cavendish stopped and plundered his ship off the coast of California. De Fuca's first attempt to find the straits failed when his soldiers mutinied, but in 1592 he was asked to try again with only one ship. He sailed north along the coast of California and beyond until he entered a broad channel which he followed as far as the 47th or 48th degree of latitude. He described the country on either side of the channel, as well as the natives dressed in furs whom he saw there. He was convinced that he had found his goal, but because he was worried about the Indians he went no farther. He expected a great reward for his accomplishment but the Viceroy had nothing but praise for him. De Fuca then returned to Spain where he again hoped to be rewarded, but his only reward was a reception by the king and public recognition. Disillusioned and broke, he went home to the island of Cephallonia.

In Venice, de Fuca met the English diplomat Michael Lok and after describing his voyages, he convinced Lok that England could use a man of his knowledge and experience in her own search for the Northwest Passage. But, while Lok was trying to make arrangements with English officials for money and ships, de Fuca died. It seems clear from the descriptions which de Fuca gave Lok that he sailed into the straits which separate Vancouver Island from the state of Washington. In 1725 the Russian Imperial Academy of Science named these straits for him, the Straits of Juan de Fuca.

The Straits of de Fuca are named for the Greek sailor who discovered them. They separate Vancouver Island from the state of Washington.

Greek names, or people with "greco" or "griego" attached to their names continue to appear in America throughout colonial times. Usually these were merchants or seafaring men such as the Captain Thomas Grecian who came to Boston from Ireland in 1660. His children had Greek names and he was probably a Greek. Unfortunately, since nothing is known of these people except their names in some public record, such clues are hard to follow further.

The first sizeable settlement of Greeks in America took place in 1767 under rather unusual circumstances. Florida had become a British colony in 1763. An enterprising Scottish doctor named Andrew Turnbull obtained permission from the governor of Florida to work 20,000 acres of uncultivated land near St. Augustine. Turnbull's wife was the daughter of a Greek general from Smyrna, and Turnbull himself was familiar with the Mediterranean area.

Mrs. Andrew Turnbull
(1726-1792)

Dr. Andrew Turnbull
(1720-1792)

Ruins of New Smyrna, the Greek-American settlement founded by the Turnbulls in Florida in 1767. It was named in honor of Mrs. Turnbull's home in Greece.

He returned there to find settlers to work his land. He collected destitute, desperate people from Greece, Italy, Corsica, and Majorca. He induced them to come with him by painting a picture of Florida as a paradise and promising to make them landowners. He brought about 1,400 men, women, and children to the settlement which he named New Smyrna in honor of his wife's home.

Under the terms of his contract with the government, Turnbull was to bring only Protestants to Florida (the Orthodox Greek Christians qualified). He had also agreed to supply them with passage, food, and clothing for three years and return passage if they wanted to leave after six months trial. In addition, he agreed to give 50 acres of land for the head of every family with an additional 25 acres for each child. The voyage was terribly hard and many of the colonists died at sea, yet even worse conditions awaited them in Florida. Instead of the vineyards and olive orchards which they had been led to expect, they found themselves cultivating cotton in swampy, malaria-infested land and being harassed by hostile Indians. Furthermore, their work was directed by English overseers who knew none of the languages spoken by the colonists and who treated them exactly as the black slaves in other southern plantations were treated. When Turnbull's promises were not kept, the settlers finally realized that they were no better than slaves. The leaders of one group which tried to escape to Cuba were executed. They might all have perished there if they had not learned accidentally that they might have legal redress. In the meantime, the governor who had granted Turnbull his charter had been replaced by another who was not on good terms with the doctor. The first colonists who left New Smyrna stole away secretly, but when they found a sympathetic government and legal help available in St. Augustine they began a mass exodus. By 1777 the New Smyrna colony was completely deserted, and the Turnbulls had gone to South Carolina. Of a total of 1,400 immigrants who were brought by Turnbull to Florida, only 600 survived the hardships, malaria, and Indians to find freedom.

The site of New Smyrna today.

6. *The Century of Revolt*

The nineteenth century was a century of revolt throughout the western world. With the examples of the successful American and French revolutions, the Spaniards, the Poles, Serbs, Greeks, and Latin American states all sought national independence in the nineteenth century. The idea of national autonomy was putting an end to empires.

The Turks had never been able (nor had they ever tried) to weld the diverse people of their empire into a nation. Each ethnic group remained individually distinct. After the conquest of Constantinople, in an effort to regain the cooperation of the Christian population, the Sultan had restored the position, rights, and privileges of the Patriarch of Constantinople over the Greek Church. He also gave him additional civil and judicial powers over the Christian population. This special position gave the church some influence with the Turkish government. It made the church a powerful force in the Greek community and had the effect of binding all Greek-speaking people closely to their church, their only channel to the Turkish government.

As the empire aged, the old vigor of the Turks declined. The later empire, after 1699, suffered from a long succession of incompetent Sultans. With enemies pressing on all sides and a government inadequate to the problems of empire, the Turks resorted to harsh, despotic methods to keep the empire functioning. Taxes became ruinous in many places. There was no machinery for the redress of grievances against local Turkish authorities. As their misery increased, the peoples of the Turkish Empire rose in revolt in scattered areas. Whenever they did, they were put down with such violence that their resistance was intensified. In Greece many escaped or were driven into the mountains where they lived as bandits waging intermittent guerilla warfare on the Turkish authorities. Among the higher classes secret revolutionary groups were formed, sometimes with the knowledge of the church. They worked to get the help of other nations and important individuals for the cause of Greek freedom. This was roughly the situation in 1821 at the beginning of the Greek War for Independence.

In America the revolution was still new. The young American government was carefully feeling its way in the world, observing strict neutrality, trying to establish commercial relations and attain recognition and representation in the countries of the world. Many of the leaders of the revolution, including Jefferson, were still alive, however, and some were still active in public life. They regarded Greece as the cradle of democracy and republicanism and felt a deep debt to the Greeks of classical times. In addition, they were almost automatically in sympathy with the efforts of any nation to be free of the old imperial powers. Because of exciting new archaeological excavations in Italy, a new interest in classical culture, both Greek and Roman, had grown up in western Europe and America. There had also been a revival of classical styles in art, architecture, and domestic design. Thus, educated Americans were unusually interested in Greece at this time. Because of their interest they were aware of the desperate condition of the modern Greeks and their desire for freedom.

The Lincoln Memorial is a prominent example of the influence of classical Greek styles on American architecture.

The Greek War for Independence was a ferocious struggle between a small guerilla style army and a larger, more conventional Turkish force. For Greece to be subdued it was necessary for the Turks to occupy the Peloponnesus, the southernmost region of Greece. Each campaigning season the Turkish Army began its march down the routes which follow either coastline, but they were hampered and harried over the rugged trails by the Greeks. Although they had more success in some years than in others, the Turkish army had never finished the job before the approach of winter forced them to withdraw to the north again.

The Greeks established a revolutionary government early in the war so that they would be prepared to assume power if Greece should drive out the Turks. But once the government was established, that old theme in Greek history, political discord, again arose. During the times when the Turks were withdrawn, the Greek military leaders fought each other over the location of the government (it moved often during these years), who should head it, who should be represented in it, and how it should be organized.

The Triple Alliance — Britain, France and Russia — gave some assistance and lots of sympathy, but since they wanted no war with Turkey themselves, they avoided an open alliance. The Greeks had great respect and affection for America and for the Americans who went to Greece to give aid as private citizens. They always expected official aid from America but though many influential friends of the Greek cause sought help in America, none ever came. The American Navy was stationed in the Mediterranean throughout the war. They observed the course of the conflict and lent unofficial aid from time to time but their secret mission was to try to establish trade with Turkey. America never changed its official position but the American public collected a total of eight shiploads of food and supplies for the civilian refugees of the war. Other American individuals served with the Greek forces or contributed other services on a private basis. These kindnesses and sacrifices built a bond of affection between Greece and America which was never forgotten. In general, the term "Philhellene" means one who loves Greece and all things Greek but the term was applied especially to the Americans (and other foreigners) who devoted themselves to the cause of Greek liberty during their War for Independence.

7. *Greek Refugees in America*

The Greeks who came to America at this time were mainly children or young men of better families, as well as orphans or refugees of the war, who were sent to America for their education by the American Philhellenes who found them in Greece. Most became successful or even eminent in their chosen work. They helped the cause of Greek-American friendship both here and abroad.

Professor Evangelinos Apostolides Sophocles was born in Thessaly. He was well launched in a career of classical scholarship when the war interrupted his studies. He continued them in Cairo and later in Syra (an island off the southern tip of Greece) with the classical scholar Gages, who gave him the nickname Sophocles because he was such a gifted student. In Syra an American missionary met him and invited him to go America. Sophocles arrived in 1828 and continued to write and study until 1842 when he joined Harvard College as a tutor in Greek. He remained a member of the Harvard faculty until his death in 1883. Harvard granted him honorary A.M. and LL.D. degrees and created a new professorship of Ancient, Byzantine, and Modern Greek for him. He also received honorary degrees from Yale and Western Reserve Universities. He wrote several grammars, but his great work was a Greek lexicon of over 1,000 pages. He lived and worked alone in the same small apartment all the years he was at Harvard. He kept house for himself and tended a flock of pet chickens which he named for friends and colleagues. He was a man whose international reputation for scholarship brought much attention to Harvard. Though he was reserved and eccentric, he was respected and loved by generations of students.

Evangelinos Apostolides Sophocles (1805-1883) scholar and educator.

Rear Admiral George Partridge Colvocoresses fought in the Spanish-American War.

In 1822 one of the most savage episodes of the War for Independence took place. Of the 100,000 Greek inhabitants of the island of Chios, all but about 5,000 were either massacred or sold into slavery by the Turks. A number of the children later sent to America were survivors of this massacre. One of these, George M. Colvocoresses (1816–1872), had a distinguished naval career as commander of the *USS Supply* and the *Saratoga* during the Civil War. He retired as a Captain. His son, George Partridge Colvocoresses, followed in his father's footsteps as a naval officer in the Spanish-American War. The son attained the rank of Rear Admiral. Several other Greek-Americans of this period also served in the American Navy.

John Zachos (1820–1898) was the child of a prominent Greek family which had held a position of importance in the Turkish government. His father was a member of a secret society plotting revolution. Though he escaped, after having been betrayed to the Turks, he was killed a short time later fighting in northern Greece. His mother managed to protect her children throughout the war, but after the war she married a man who was an official in the new Greek government. Later, she was persuaded to send her son to America to be educated. He was trained as a physician but he never practiced medicine. Instead he worked at various educational tasks. He was co-principal of a girl's academy in Ohio for a while. After the Civil War he became administrator for Paris Island where he supervised the welfare and education of some 600 Negro "refugees" who had been collected there after they were left destitute by their former masters. Later Zachos served as a minister and then as a professor of rhetoric. In 1871 his friend Peter Cooper asked him to become curator of the Cooper Union, an institute for the advancement of arts and sciences, in New York City. He continued to serve the Union as lecturer and literary head for the rest of his life.

The home of Colonel Lucas Miltiades Miller, on Lake Winnebago in Oshkosh, Wisconsin, 1880. Miller was elected to the House of Representatives in 1890.

Dr. Samuel Gridley Howe (1801-1876), a prominent American supporter of the Greek revolution and a patron of Greek refugees.

Michael Anagnos (1837-1906), a Greek journalist who came to work with Dr. Howe in America.

Colonel Lucas Miltiades Miller (1824-1902) was a war orphan who was adopted by the American Colonel J. P. Miller who fought with the Greek forces. He was educated in the law and shortly after he was admitted to the bar he moved to Oshkosh, Wisconsin. He became a farmer there and took an active part in public affairs. He was a colonel during the Mexican War. After the war he was elected a Representative from Wisconsin to Congress in 1891

One of the greatest American Philhellenes was Dr. Samuel Gridley Howe (1801–1876). He served as surgeon to the Greek Army, helped distribute the relief cargo sent to aid the Greek civilian refugees, and established hospitals in the new nation. In addition to the time he spent in Greece between the years 1825 and 1831, he wrote and traveled in America to try to encourage Americans to aid the Greek cause. After the war he pioneered in the field of education for the blind: he established the Perkins

31

Institute in Boston. Later, in 1861, Howe returned to Greece during the Cretan Revolution to direct the relief assistance for the Cretans. He hired as his secretary Michael Anagnos (1837–1906), a young Greek journalist, who eventually returned to America with him. Later, Howe hired him as a teacher in the Institute. Anagnos married Howe's only daughter and, when Howe retired, he became director of the Institute. Under his direction, the Institute took increased interest in the deaf blind. Miss Ann Sullivan, the tutor who first helped Helen Keller, was sent to her from the Perkins Institute. His programs for the blind were most progressive for his time: he established a kindergarten for the blind, began a press for printing books for the blind, saw that they were distributed throughout the libraries of Massachusetts, and helped develop programs for training the blind in self-supporting trades and occupations. Anagnos was also well-known for the help he gave to Greek immigrants, his participation in the Greek community in Boston, and the efforts he made to help improve education in Greece.

8. *Postwar Problems and the Reasons for the Great Wave*

The task of restoring peace and order to the little peninsula looked insurmountable. The military leaders of the revolutionary forces who inherited the job of organizing a government had no experience, and they mistrusted the only Greeks with administrative experience, those who had been part of the Turkish government. They disagreed about everything from who should be represented to who should lead the new government. The country was devastated by the war and deeply in debt to the countries of the Triple Alliance. In the end the Greeks agreed to accept a foreign king to be chosen by the European powers. A Bavarian prince, Otho, was selected. Otho was young, inexperienced, and ignorant of Greece and her problems. He and the flock of Bavarian advisors who came with him not only did nothing to solve the country's postwar problems but actually made things worse. In 1843 Otho was forced to accept a constitution by a bloodless revolution. The constitution allowed a representative government and curbed some of the worst abuses of royal power, but it could not make up for the lack of a progressive government which could deal with the pressing problems facing the nation.

In 1867 Otho was deposed; George I of Denmark took his place. George allowed his Greek ministers to govern the country. At last the real work of reconstruction began but it was too little and too late to prevent the first large exodus of people from Sparta in the 1870's and 1880's.

The 400-year Turkish occupation had brought no improvements, reforms, or progress to the whole of Greece. The country re-entered the western world in the nineteenth century very much as it had left it in the fifteenth. When, in the last decades of the nineteenth century, the government's attempts to modernize the country began to bring some prosperity, it was the urban middle-class which gained by it. New railroads, a new navy, and new industry all meant progress and growth for the cities. However, the depressed rural majority—for Greece was mainly an agricultural country—suffered on without even a forum for its grievances. The old unjust land laws were never reformed, but taxes were collected in the same unjust ways as always and, as always, the rural population carried an unfair share of the tax burden. While cities and railroads were being built, vital country roads were not even repaired. Most of the country's financial capital was being invested in the great new modernization projects so that very little money remained available in rural areas. Money for loans was available only at such high rates that no farmer could afford to borrow to improve his farm or increase his production. Under these conditions, once a man got into debt, he had little chance of getting out. Caught in this financial squeeze, farmers had less chance of being able to educate their sons or to provide dowries for their daughters. Without the possibility of education or good marriages for his children, the farmer lost his only hope for bettering his family. He could look forward only to a life of frustration and despair. In addition, any natural disaster, such as an earthquake, drought, floods, or any change in the usual markets for their produce, brought complete ruin to many farmers.

When the Triple Alliance was making the settlements at the end of the War for Independence, the Greeks were given control over the smallest possible part of the Greek peninsula. This left more Greeks outside of Greece than inside Greece. The Ionian islands were under British protectorate, the Aegean islands under Italian control. Almost everything else, northern Greece (Thessaly, Epiros, Macedonia), Crete, Cyprus, and the coastal area of Anatolia including Smyrna and Constantinople itself, were still in Turkish territory. These lands outside Greek sovereignty were known as "unredeemed lands." The Greek government soon made the recovery of these lands part of its permanent policy but the political parties differed as to how it could be done. At one end of the scale were those who modestly hoped that the control of predominantly Greek territories might be restored to Greece in time, by diplomatic means. At the other end of the scale were those who dreamed of restoring the old Byzantine Empire and returning Greece to her ancient glory, by military means if necessary. The continual threat of Turkey and a number of wars beginning with the Greco-Turkish War in 1897 forced Greece to maintain a state of military readiness. Many families suffered additional hardship when their adult men were pressed into military service.

Heavy, unjust taxation, scarce money, natural disasters, market failures, and threat of military service weighed most heavily on the rural poor. All of these things combined in various ways, year after year, to leave Greek farmers without any opportunity to improve their lot or any hope for the future. So, in 1875, when Christos Tsankonas came back to Sparta from his first trip to America his fellow countrymen were ready to listen to what he had to say.

When he returned to the United States, five of his countrymen went with him. In the decade between 1871–1880, 210 Greeks left for America. In the next 10 years 2,308 followed them. The great flight from Greece had begun.

A major cause for Greek immigration was the poverty of the rural people.

An unusual photograph of Greek immigrants in costume for
International Night. Lowell, Massachusetts, 1925.

PART II

The Immigrants

1. *Motives and Expectations*

Who were these Greeks who chose to gamble everything on a
chance in America? As we have seen, the economic and political
problems of Greece had their severest effects on the rural citizens.
Men left with so little opportunity responded with eagerness and
courage to a new hope. The emigrants were usually in the produc-
tive years of their lives. Between 1880 and 1902, 95% were males.
Most of them had family responsibilities and some small resources
in the form of land, livestock, or modest savings. They were men
of the soil with no special skills and usually only a minimum of
education. Their intentions were clear and simple. They wanted to
earn enough money to solve their financial problems, and they were
willing to exile themselves temporarily to do it. Most Greeks,
then and now, at home and abroad, love their country and are in-
tensely loyal to it. The fact that they left Greece did not mean that
they forsook it. They left behind wives, parents, and children.
When their debts were paid and they had saved a little to make life
more comfortable, it was their intention to go home again.

Generally, those who left Greece had some personal information on which to base their decision to emigrate. Usually this had come to them in the form of letters from relatives or friends. Most immigrants tried to send money home as soon as they could—even if it meant borrowing a sum to enclose in their first letters. So, although there were plenty of letters from those suffering hardship and unhappiness in America, these were more than offset by encouraging, positive, and hopeful letters—especially when they contained cash. When emigration reached its full flow the Greek government and newspapers published letters and other documents describing the miseries of the immigrants in the hope that they could discourage emigration. The men of Greece were not to be denied, however. Most of them began their great adventure knowing that they might fail but insisting on their right to try. They found passage money in any way they could: mortgaged their land, sold their livestock, used their savings, or borrowed from friends or relatives.

Although village life in Greece was hard, it had the age-old order of family, friends, church, coffeehouse, work, and holiday. Nothing in this life, nothing which friends or relatives could convey in letters could possible prepare the emigrants for the life they would face in America.

The great movement began in the region around Sparta. From 1890 to 1910 an estimated three-fourths of the male population between the ages of 18 and 35 left Sparta; some went to the United States, others to destinations in Russia, Egypt, Turkey, or central Africa. After 1890 emigrants came from all over Greece. Those who left Turkish lands usually did so for political reasons. When the new Turkish constitution of 1908 required military service of Greek citizens, many left to avoid serving in the Turkish army.

A failure in the price of currants, a major product of Greece, caused more to leave in the 1890's. Earthquakes, droughts, and economic problems in Greece as well as economic recessions and the Spanish-American War in the United States caused the current of emigration to ebb and flow, but after 1890 it had become a tide which could not be turned back.

Although finding passage money may have been difficult in some cases, it was only the beginning of the troubles which many Greeks faced in their pursuit of a new life in America. Greeks were free to leave their own country without restriction, but many were turned back after they reached the United States because they could not pass the physical requirements for entry. Since the Greek government would not allow American health officials to operate in Greece, the steamship companies had lost money on the emigrants who were turned back. Therefore, they ultimately provided health and other types of inspection for those who purchased tickets so that entry became reasonably certain.

Unlike many European immigrants who had been drawn to America by the promise of free land, practically no Greeks became farmers in spite of their agricultural backgrounds. Since they usually planned a limited stay in America, very few were interested in the long term investments of time and money required for farming. They went straight to the cities where they could find the help and companionship of other Greeks and the jobs and wages they sought.

Immigrants leaving for the United States at Patras, Greece, early 1900's.

2. *Obstacles in America*

Language

The new arrival nearly always had the name of a city and friends or relatives who were prepared to help him when he reached them. He was warmly welcomed as a newcomer from home but the problems which quickly followed his arrival were all but overwhelming. Most acute was the matter of language. Very few had any preparation in English at all. The vast difference between the two languages made it impossible for Greek-speaking people to pick up English quickly. Most newcomers had to rely on their countrymen who had been here longer and who might know more, but often very little more, than those they were trying to help.

Lack of Skills

When it came to finding a job, the language barrier was a great handicap. In many cases it forced the immigrant to take the simplest kind of manual labor. But, even if they had been more fluent, most immigrants, coming as they did from rural backgrounds, had no skills and would have had to work as unskilled laborers anyway. They began their hard climb to prosperity as railroad construction and maintenance workers, as day laborers, dishwashers, and bootblacks, or as street peddlers of fruits, vegetables, flowers, cigars, or candy. These last occupations sometimes provided a start for those who wanted to be in business. Very little cash was needed to begin as a bootblack or peddler. By working harder than his competition and allowing himself only the bare necessities of life, the successful Greek was able to save enough to acquire a shop of his own. In the early 1900's in Chicago, there seemed to be a Greek candy store at every other corner.

A large number of Greeks engaged in fishing in New England, Florida, and California, though the size of this group did not grow in proportion to the number of immigrants. During the recession of 1893 many Greeks were forced out of peddling and into the textile mills of New England where they did very well. A few professional people, especially doctors and lawyers, came to the United States but they too found the language barrier a fierce handicap. Whatever the job, however, only the worst poverty could interrupt the flow of cash to those at home. The funds sent home were meant, first of all, to settle family debts, then perhaps to provide dowries or to pay passage for some other member of the family, and finally to be invested in the home neighborhood. A study of emigration made by the Greek government in 1906 showed that districts from which emigration was heaviest had become the most prosperous because of the money which the emigrants were sending home. Until the Balkan Wars (1912–1913) it had not been necessary for Greece to restrict the emigration of men of military age, for the government did not want to interfere with this important source of income from which the whole country benefited. The Greek government kept no records of the number of Greeks who emigrated

Front page from the *Omaha Daily News*. Anti-Greek sentiment erupted into a riot in Omaha in 1909.

before World War I. American records are confused because Greeks living in Turkish territory sometimes counted themselves as Greeks, sometimes as Turks. Therefore, it is not possible to know precisely the extent of immigration before World War II, but the best modern estimates suggest that a figure of 500,000 is likely.

Prejudice and Hostility

Greek immigrants soon found that they had to take a place at the bottom of the immigrant ladder. Other immigrant groups though here for only a slightly longer time were still in a position to harass and ridicule the Greeks. Because they knew so little English and were ignorant of American law and customs they were fair game for anyone who wanted to trick them. There were countless schemes for doing this. Whenever the economy slumped in America, people who could find no other reason for their financial troubles were happy to blame them on a group of strangers. If there was any shortage of jobs, the native labor force did not want to share the work with alien laborers. The fact that the Greeks were latecomers and had more than a little trouble with English meant that they often knew nothing of the goals and methods of labor unions. The Greeks sometimes offended organized labor by acting as strike breakers or by providing a whole new supply of cheap labor in some industries.

Greeks faced all kinds of discrimination and opposition from snubs and insults to violent anti-Greek riots. A severe disturbance took place in Omaha in 1909: the Greek community of about 1,200 was driven from the city and its property destroyed. Of course, every large group which entered the United States experienced much the same treatment, though that would have been no comfort to the Greeks even if they had realized it. They were proud of their homeland and heritage and were anxious to correct the false opinions and unjust treatment which were so prevalent.

Padrones

Even harder to bear were the injustices which Greek immigrants suffered at the hands of their countrymen. As the numbers of Greeks in America grew, some of the more successful, following the example of American business, began to organize their enterprises into chains. Greeks had managed to succeed in the shoeshining business largely because they were willing to work harder and longer for smaller returns than their competitors. When a few began organizing chains of shoeshine parlors, their profits depended on a large supply of very cheap labor. The *padrone* system which was used to supply this labor also existed among other immigrant groups. The laborers obtained by these padrones were really indentured servants similar to those common in America in colonial times. The same system was used to recruit railroad labor and peddlers as well as bootblacks. Of course this "contract labor" was illegal but the padrones had many ways of getting around the law.

The padrone or employer found his victims by contacting friends and relatives in Greece. Many families were anxious to have their young sons, 14 to 18 years of age, go to America but were too poor to send them and too poor to provide any opportunity or education at home. The padrones offered to provide passage and transportation plus a small amount of cash (usually just enough to get the boy admitted) in return for his services for a specified time — anywhere from three months to one year. During this time the boy received board and room and was expected to work long hard hours. The living provided was usually as meager as possible and the work left the boys with no time or energy for recreation or school. Even though they received only passage money, the families of these boys had to give a guarantee equal to one year's wages to prevent them from breaking their contracts. Most families had to mortgage their property to provide such a guarantee.

After a year, the boys began to work at salaries of 10 to 20 dollars a year. They might eventually average between 110 and 180

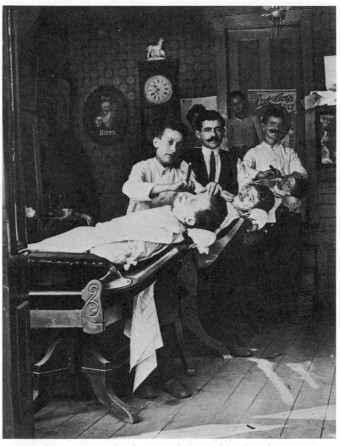

A rare photograph of a Greek-owned barbershop, 1910.

dollars a year. Neither the boys nor their families were aware that anything was wrong with these arrangements. The families were happy to have the opportunity for their sons and considered the padrones their benefactors. Because the boys knew no English and depended upon the padrones for every kind of advice and information it was easy enough to keep them ignorant. In addition, the pitiful salaries offered by the padrones seemed very desirable to impoverished families whose sons had no better prospects in Greece and who had no idea of American customs or values.

Gradually American opinion was roused against this system. Laws were passed which were meant to stop the practice and punish the padrones, who of course then devised many crafty ways of escaping prosecution. Several factors finally worked together to bring the ugly system to an end. Many of the boys slowly learned enough to realize that they were being exploited and found better jobs on their own. Changing shoe styles and the increased use of automobiles brought a decline in the volume of business. Aid societies were formed to help the bootblacks obtain better conditions; eventually they even organized unions. Undoubtedly the increased understanding and independence of the immigrants themselves was the most important factor in putting the padrones out of business.

Alienation

For each Greek probably the greatest problem of all was his feeling of loneliness and loss while working in a strange society. Though he hoped for a place in American life, he wanted it as a Greek. If he had children he also wanted them to learn the Greek language and something about the homeland and cultural heritage of their parents.

3. A Variety of Solutions

Greek Brotherhoods

Like other immigrants, the Greeks gathered together in the cities where they could hope to find some security among their countrymen. As one friend and relative followed another, these colonies of Greeks soon grew so large that some kind of organization seemed necessary to help the compatriots solve their problems. The first organizations formed by Greeks when they met far from home tended to be brotherhoods or fraternities of those who came from the same town or village in Greece. These groups served as social clubs and as self-help societies. Because each small fraternity had a full set of officers, uniforms, and banners and took part in all parades and civic functions, members gained some prestige and a sense of importance which they could not find elsewhere. These clubs raised funds for projects in their hometowns. They might help build a school, hospital, or bridge, provide relief after an earthquake, or help widows and orphans. Often the priest or someone else from home would write to the members asking for help with a particular problem. However, the contribution these groups could make was limited by the spirit of localism which governed their activities. They often wasted their efforts in dispute with rival societies.

In the hope of coordinating the activities of all Greek societies, The *Panhellenic Union* was formed in 1907. But soon this society found conflict in its ranks. One side believed the Union should help the Greek government reclaim the "unredeemed" lands. The other side wanted the society to help Greek immigrants help themselves in America, although they had no objection to helping Greeks at home on a personal basis. Something new was added to the quarrel when a minister from Greece became the head of the Panhellenic Union. He had been sent to see that the group did what was of most use to the Greek government. When rumors

A group of Greek men relax with their instruments, Lowell, Massachusetts, 1919. Both formal and informal fraternal organizations were popular among the Greek-Americans.

A picnic in Lowell, Massachusetts, 1920. The men are about to perform a traditional Greek dance.

began that the Greek government intended to tax the Greeks in America, the immigrants refused to be directed by foreign officials and would not cooperate. Even after the Union rid itself of foreign leadership it continued to be more interested in the old country than in the new.

After the first World War more and more immigrants realized that America would be their permanent home and larger numbers became naturalized, some as a result of serving in the American army during the war. Many immigrants who had returned to Greece to fight in the Balkan War came back to America after the war with their families and intended to stay. But their position was still uncomfortable in many ways. America became increasingly isolationist after the war; aliens were still not welcome.

The *American Hellenic Educational Progressive Association* (AHEPA) was founded in 1922 to advance the Americanization of

Greeks and to help combat unfavorable publicity and propaganda about them. The organization took the form of a fraternity. Its official language was English. No special attention was given to the Orthodox Church. In fact, many AHEPA members belonged to churches of other denominations.

For those who felt that AHEPA catered too much to the anti-foreign feeling then prevalent in America, there was a new organization to join in the next year, 1923. The *Greek American Progressive Association* (GAPA) also assumed that the Greek immigrants were in America to stay. But their main concern was the Greek heritage, Greek language, and support for the Greek Church in reaction to the policy of AHEPA which seemed to be abandoning these things. Although GAPA appealed to older and more conservative Greeks, it was never able to match the membership of AHEPA.

Church

Of more immediate value to the Greek immigrant community was the organization of the *kinotitos* or community council. This was a governing body which was to provide for the establishment and financing of church and school, and to oversee the election of officials and the hiring and firing of priests, teachers, and janitors. This body was formed after a community reached a population of 500.

Because of the importance of the Orthodox Church as the center of community life in Greece, the establishment of a church was one of the first projects of interest to the Greek communities in America. Funds were given by people whose incomes were already stretched thin. Places of worship were either found or built, first in New York and Chicago in the early 1890's. These remained the only two regular churches during this decade. Others which were founded were served by traveling priests. Between 1907 and 1909 churches were established in 10 more cities and, in the period 1914 to 1918, 61 more were organized. By the end of World

War I, 130 Greek Orthodox Churches were in existence. Of course there was a shortage of trained clergymen. Priests were brought from Greece but often they were ignorant and unequal to the duties of a city parish. Even those who were well educated and of better social background were often unable to adjust to American life or to give the kind of help the immigrant congregation needed.

The Eastern Orthodox Church is divided into several independent national churches, such as the Russian, Bulgarian, Cypriote, and Greek. Each has its own Metropolitan or Patriarch but all are presided over by the supreme pontiff, the Ecumenical Patriarch of Constantinople. Naturally, the Greeks in America wanted to be part of the Greek Church. Unfortunately the Greek hierarchy paid very little attention to the American church. Their representatives did not understand American problems or please Americans. It was not until 1918 that the American church even had a bishop. Before this time much business of the American church had to be carried on through bishops in Greece. The American church wanted and needed a workable administrative organization, jurisdiction over its own church, and facilities for educating its own clergy. The quarrels which developed over these issues went on year after year and cost the church much support.

Annunciation Church, Milwaukee. This modern Greek Orthodox church was designed by Frank Lloyd Wright.

Athenagoras, the Ecumenical
Patriarch of Constantinople.

Iakovos, Archbishop of
North and South America.

Finally, in 1930 the Ecumenical Patriarch took notice of the
sad state of the American church. Passing over all the quarreling
bishops and rival clergymen, he chose Athenagoras, the Metropolitan of Corfu, to become the Archbishop of North and South
America. Athenagoras began to reorganize administrative practices
and settle questions of jurisdiction which had been causing trouble
for decades. He eliminated the other dioceses and made all the
bishops directly responsible to him. He gave the clergy jurisdiction over such matters as the hiring of priests and over all spiritual
affairs. To make the Greek schools more successful, he tried to reorganize them with the church as the sponsoring organization.

Athenagoras also encouraged the churches to take drastic steps
to deal with the financial difficulties caused by the depression. He
is responsible for lifting the Greek Church in America from a mire
of dissension and disorder and giving it its identity as an American
institution. The great importance attained by the American church
was acknowledged when Athenagoras was elected Ecumenical
Patriarch of Constantinople in 1948. Now in his eighties he is still
pursuing his ecumenical goals throughout Christendom. The
present Archbishop of North and South America is Iakovos.

Greek Schools

The Greek schools were organized to provide the children of Greek immigrants with a knowledge of the language and culture their parents regarded so highly. The Greeks found, as did other immigrant groups with similar ambitions, that it was an uphill struggle. Qualified teachers were hard to find, as were funds with which to pay them. The children often resented attending Greek classes after their regular school day was over and they resisted anything that seemed old-fashioned or strange or set them apart from their American friends. This was particularly true during periods of anti-Greek feeling. Gradually, against their wishes but in spite of anything they could do, the children born of immigrants in America became Americans.

Holy Cross Chapel at Panhellenic University, near Boston, Massachusetts.

Greek Language Papers

The daily newspaper is a vital part of life in Greece and it was inevitable that community life in America should give rise to Greek language newspapers. Many began as scandal or gossip sheets and had short lives. But there were a large number of well-run and adequately financed papers which survived because they filled a pressing need for information among the immigrants. They also provided an opportunity to read Greek in a current and correct form. They formed a link, in the early days, between the Greek and English-speaking communities. Notices and information of various kinds could be made available to people who could not read English. Greek language papers also published much more news of Greece than was available elsewhere and provided American Greeks with material for their endless debates over Greek politics. These papers were an important link with home for the immigrant. They also helped in many cases to educate the immigrants in American customs.

Atlantis, founded in New York by Solon Vlasto in 1894, survived longer than any other paper and became a daily in 1904. It took a strictly Royalist position and was somewhat ruthless in its treatment of papers which tried to take the opposite view. In 1915 the first successful liberal paper, the *National Herald (Ethnikos Kyrix),* was founded. Demetrios Callimachos, who served as editor for 27 years, provided a voice for the liberal point of view and was an important force in shaping opinion in the Greek population. *Greek Star (Helenikos Astir)* a Chicago paper founded in 1904 is still published. Almost all large Greek communities had a Greek language paper at least for a time.

The Royalist-Venizelist debate in Greece divided the Greek-Americans into two political camps. It first became important to Americans before the first World War when the nations were choosing sides in the growing conflict. King Constantine of Greece had been educated in Germany, he had a German wife, and he did not wish to offend Germany. He and his political friends wanted Greece to stay out of the war and remain completely neutral. The liberal party in Greece, led by Prime Minister Venizelos, wanted Greece to enter the war on the side of the Allies. America, of course, favored the Allies even before she entered the war. From this time on most Greek-Americans considered themselves either Royalists or Venizelists in political affairs both in Greece and America. The Royalists tended to take the Republican side in American politics and to prefer the aims of GAPA and be strong supporters of the Orthodox Church. Venizelists or Liberals favored the Democratic side usually and the policies of AHEPA, and were less concerned with church affairs. With *Atlantis* and the *National Herald* leading the way, the Greeks in America argued each political problem in Greece from these two points of view.

Solon Vlasto (1852-1927) founded the first daily Greek-American newspaper, *Atlantis,* in 1894.

In 1915, **Demetrios Callimachos** founded the *National Herald,* the first successful liberal Greek-American paper.

Greek *taverna* on the island of Rhodes. Men come to the *tavernas* and coffee houses to relax, talk, smoke, and play games.

Coffeehouses

For the newly arrived immigrants, far from home and family, with very little to spend on diversions, life could be very drab and lonely. Some of the men lived together; several would occupy a whole house and take turns with housekeeping and cooking. Since most of them were convinced of the superiority of Greek womanhood and planned to marry only Greek women, they avoided the company of American women.

The coffeehouses which were established in Greek neighborhoods were the logical solution to the problems of finding company and entertainment for these men. A familiar institution in Greece, a coffeehouse was inexpensive both to operate and to patronize. Here, for the price of a cup of thick Greek coffee, a man (and men only) could sit at a small table smoking, reading his paper, or talking politics and reminiscing with friends for as long as he wished. Such a place filled a large gap in the lives of many lonely men.

Music by the patrons, dancing, and cards could be added to the amusements available in the coffeehouses. Eventually, those in the larger cities could offer some other modest entertainments. Traveling players of the shadow plays familiar in the old country performed in the coffeehouses. Sometimes strong men, musicians, or dancers were available. Usually the proprietor gave these performers board, room, and a small sum and they were allowed to keep whatever the customers gave them after the performance. But the coffeehouses attracted critics. They were a strange institution and no doubt many non-Greeks misunderstood the violent political arguments they overheard there. Gambling became a problem in a few of the houses and others suffered from the bad image this created. Many probably objected for the same reasons they objected to billiard parlors—a rather vague feeling that the places were unsavory. Eventually, as the lives of the Greeks became more normal, the family became the center of social life and with less need for them and opposition from other parts of the community, the coffeehouses began to disappear.

PART III

The Greek Achievement

Slowly, in spite of the fact that they had no training or experience, Greeks began to prosper in business. Their first successes were in shoeshine parlors, candy stores, and restaurants. As commerce brought Greeks into the main current of American business life, they were quick to try enterprises of all kinds.

1. *Repatriation*

Of course, not all Greeks succeeded. Some continued to live in poverty. Some returned to Greece without either money or health. Before World War II a fairly large proportion of Greek immigrants had gone back to Greece to live. Of those who came between 1908 and 1931, about 40% returned to Greece, mostly before 1925. They were repatriated for several different reasons and in several different ways. Some simply carried out their plan of improving their fortunes in order to return home. Many of these were able to make important contributions to Greek life. For instance, the first pasteurization plant in Athens was begun by a man who had learned the business and purchased his equipment in the United States. Others used "know-how" they had acquired in America to solve problems in their towns and villages. Some, even those who were living quite comfortably, found that they missed certain comforts and conveniences which they had grown used to in America.

Because of confusion in the laws regulating immigrants, some Greeks who planned to stay in America were drafted into the Greek army while they were visiting at home and never managed to get back again. Some who had gone back for a visit married women who did not want to leave Greece. So Greeks were repatriated for many reasons. Some remembered America fondly as a place where they would be if they could. Others remembered only that they had never worked so hard or been so miserable as they were in America.

2. *Survival of Hellenic Culture*

The first World War was a turning point for many immigrants. The postwar years were prosperous ones. Many Greeks earned their citizenship by service in the American army. There were many things that worked to Americanize the Greek immigrant — the anti-foreign feeling after the war, the constant discussion in the Greek community about Americanization, and the work of such organizations as AHEPA. In addition, many of these families had growing children who were American citizens and who did not want to be set apart in any way. A high point of naturalization was reached in the late 1920's.

Hermes Social Club, dedicated to the preparation of Greek immigrants for American citizenship.

The second generation, children of immigrants, who didn't want to be different from other Americans, tended to reject their parents' attempts to "Hellenize" them. Even parents who only hoped that their children would keep their Greek names, their religion, and learn the Greek language were often disappointed. Many changed or Americanized their names. A large number left the Greek church for others, or for none at all. More and more married Americans with each passing decade. Very few learned more than a little "household" Greek. A large number proceeded, in the face of many difficulties, to get more education and enter a variety of professions. Most of them avoided following the occupations of their fathers.

3. *Contributions to American Society*

Greek immigrants and their descendants, by their personal industry and success as individuals and by becoming good citizens, have made a generous contribution to American life. There are also many, who, because of their unique gifts and efforts, are recognized as some of our most outstanding citizens.

Spiro Agnew was elected Vice-President of the United States in 1968. From 1966 to 1968 he served as the Republican governor of the state of Maryland.

Three other Greek-Americans on the national political scene represented their states in Congress in 1967: John Brademas, Democrat of Indiana; Nicholas Galifianakis, Democrat of North Carolina; and Peter Kyros, Republican of Maine. Two major American cities, St. Paul, Minnesota, and San Francisco, have had Greek mayors in recent years. George Vavoulis was Republican mayor of St. Paul from 1960 to 1966. George Christopher, an immigrant, was Republican mayor of San Francisco from 1955 to 1964. He was defeated by Ronald Reagan in an attempt to win the Republican nomination for governor of California.

John Brademas
congressman from Indiana

Nick Galifianakis
congressman from North Carolina

Spiro Agnew (center) on the campaign trail, November 1968.

Although Greeks are active in all kinds and at all levels of American business, perhaps the two best known for their great success and their philanthropies are Spyros Skouras and Thomas Pappas.

The Skouras brothers—Charles, Spyros, and George—came to America from the Peloponnesus. They worked at menial jobs until, in 1914, they had saved enough to buy their first theatre. By 1926 they owned 37 theatres in and around St. Louis. Spyros studied finance, real estate, and theatre management. When the brothers sold their theatres to Warner Brothers, Spyros stayed on as an executive. From this time on he rose steadily until he became head of Twentieth Century Fox in 1943. Spyros and his brothers did much to aid the relief efforts for Greece during and after World War II.

Spyros Skouras
executive director of 20th Century Fox films

Thomas A. Pappas
director of the Standard Oil industrial complex in Greece

Thomas Pappas came to America as a child. Beginning with his father's grocery store, Pappas built up a chain of 35 stores with importing and wholesaling sidelines. After the second World War he sold these interests and invested in a great variety of enterprises. With Standard Oil Company of New Jersey as a partner, Pappas is overseeing the construction of a 200-million dollar industrial complex in Thessaloniki, Greece. The eight companies of the complex will produce everything from petroleum products to steel and will make Greece self-sufficient in many of these products as well as revitalizing the economy of northern Greece.

In the performing arts the scene has become thoroughly cosmopolitan since World War II. Such films as *Topkapi* and *Zorba, the Greek* are truly international efforts with a Greek-American emphasis. Melina Mercouri, the Greek film star who was introduced to America in the film *Never on Sunday,* has worked on the New York stage and may be considered a political refugee. While all of this adds to the interest and excitement of the theatrical world, it also adds to the confusion.

In music the acknowledged master was the great symphony conductor Dimitri Mitropoulos (1896-1960), who came to the United States in 1936. He conducted the Minneapolis Symphony from 1936 to 1949 and the New York Philharmonic Orchestra until 1958. Before his death he established a fund to be used to aid young conductors.

Maria Callas, one of the world's foremost dramatic coloratura sopranos, was born in New York. She was trained in Greece and Italy and made her debut in Verona. Her years with the New York Metropolitan Opera Company, her feuds with general manager Rudolph Bing, and the virtuosity of her performances in such technically complex roles as that of Lucia in *Lucia di Lammermoor* are legendary. Since that time she has renounced her American citizenship.

Irene Dalis, a California born mezzo-soprano, made her American debut at the Metropolitan Opera in 1957. She became a leading mezzo-soprano at the Met in the following year.

Maria Callas

Dimitri Mitropoulos

Ike Pappas
CBS News Correspondent

Elia Kazan
novelist and director of movies and plays

In the field of theatre and film, one of the foremost names is doubtless that of Elia Kazan who has been a director of both stage and screen drama. He has been an innovator in the American movie industry, often using controversial themes for his films. Some of his greatest are: *A Tree Grows in Brooklyn,* 1945, *Streetcar Named Desire,* 1951, *Viva Zapata,* 1952, *America America,* 1964, and the two for which he won Academy Awards—*Gentlemen's Agreement,* 1947, and *On the Waterfront,* 1954. In 1967, Kazan published a novel, *The Arrangement,* which was well received by critics and the reading public.

John Cassavetes is a younger actor and director who has appeared in both films and television. He has experimented with an improvisational method of directing in which no scripts are used and the actors supply the dialogue as they go along.

Another personality well-known in recent years is George Maharis. He has appeared on the New York stage, in films, and on television where he played the role of Buzz Murdock for several seasons in the *Route 66* series. He won an Emmy for this portrayal in 1962.

Still another young actor who is often seen in films and on national television is George Chakiris.

The face of Ike Pappas, television reporter, is seen nearly every day on the CBS evening news.

In the sports world a list of those at the top of their profession would have to include several Greek-Americans. Milt Pappas, who was a pitcher with the Baltimore Orioles for 10 years (1958–1968), is with the Cincinnati Reds. Gus Triandos, a veteran catcher, is with the Philadelphia Phillies. In professional football, Bill George is a linebacker with the Los Angeles Rams. Alex Karras, twice All-American, is a defensive tackle with the Detroit Lions.

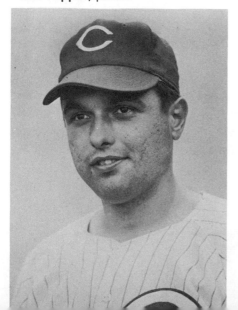

Milt Pappas, pitcher

Alex Karras
All-Pro defensive tackle

Dr. George Papanicolaou (1895-1963) developed the Pap test for the early detection of cancer.

Greek-Americans make a liberal contribution in the laboratories and classrooms of our country. In medicine, the well-known *Pap test* reminds us of the great physician, Dr. George Papanicolaou (1895-1963). While doing cancer research at the Cornell Medical Center, Dr. Papanicolaou developed a smear test for detecting cervical cancer in women. The test is simple and inexpensive and makes an early diagnosis possible, thereby saving many lives.

Nick Christophilos is a scientist whose work at the University of California at Berkeley may lead to a way to control thermonuclear reactions by using high-energy electrons.

Well-known in academic circles are the following scholars, all of whom are immigrants. Moody Erasmus Prior is a professor of English Literature of the seventeenth and eighteenth centuries and a well-known Shakespeare scholar. He is now Dean of Graduate Study at Northwestern University. Peter Charanis is Professor of Byzantine History at Rutgers University and has been largely responsible for the growth of interest in Byzantine studies in America. Dimitri Tselos is Professor of Art History specializing

Archaeologist **George Mylonas** was active in excavations at Mycenae.

in Byzantine, Early Medieval, and Modern art. He has taught at New York University, Vassar, and Bryn Mawr and is at the University of Minnesota. All of these men were trained in the United States. Another, George Mylonas, Professor at Washington University in St. Louis is a famous archaeologist who has been active in the excavations at Mycenae and Eleusis. He has published much material concerning these two sites and archaeology in general.

In the arts, three painters who are highly respected in the contemporary art world are John Xceron, William Baziotes, and Theodore Stamos. Xceron, the oldest of the three, is an immigrant who worked in Paris during the exciting days of the 1920's and whose work reflects his European experience. William Baziotes and Theodore Stamos are younger contemporaries whose work is primarily abstract expressionist in style. Both were born in the United States.

John Vassos is an industrial designer who has given form to a wide variety of products over the years. He has also painted murals and designed the United States pavilion for the Indian trade fair in New Delhi, 1955.

Harry Petrakis is a novelist who writes about the life of Greeks in Chicago from first hand experience. His latest novel, *Dream of Kings* published in 1967, has been received favorably in literary circles.

Harry Mark Petrakis, novelist and short story writer.

United States Pavilion at the trade fair in New Delhi, India, 1955. Designed by John Vassos.

4. *Contributions in War*

The reputation of Greeks as warriors is an ancient and heroic one, and Greek-Americans have been true to this tradition. During the Spanish-American War 500 Cretans volunteered to serve as a unit in Cuba if America would provide passage for them. Their offer was refused even though it was meant as an expression of gratitude for the help Americans gave Greece during their War for Independence. During the Balkan Wars (1912–1913) national feeling ran high among Greek-Americans and an amazing number volunteered to fight in Greece. Military units organized all over the United States and trained together. The Panhellenic Union acted as a recruiting agent and offended many people who thought it was improper for a foreign government to recruit in America. A total of 45,000 American volunteers served in the Balkan Wars.

The political problems in Greece and her late entry into World War I meant that Greeks in America who wanted to serve would join the American army. The Greek government tried to arrange to have Greek nationals serve as a unit under the Greek flag but America would accept no such arrangement; all aliens had to serve as individuals. A great many of them did. A definite count is not available but a good estimate based on the number of Greeks then living in the United States is about 60,000. George Dilboy was awarded the Congressional Medal of Honor after his heroic death in the first World War. In addition, Greeks contributed 30 million dollars in liberty bonds.

In 1936 a military dictator, General Metaxas (1871–1941), came to power in Greece. Most Greek-Americans were dismayed at this development in Greece especially at a time when Mussolini in Italy and Hitler in Germany were beginning to show their intentions. However, another faction in America supported Metaxas because it felt that only such a strong government could deal with the problems of Greece. Both factions made serious efforts to win the sympathy and the support of the American Greeks. The questions were discussed in America since there was a strong interest in the fate of Greece. However, the American community soon made it clear that it would have nothing to do with a pro-axis Greece and that its loyalty and interest were with America.

When the Italians marched into Greece in 1940, everything changed. Metaxas and his successor led the Greeks in resisting the Italians, and by using their old methods of mountain warfare they were driving them back when the great blow fell. In 1941,

General Metaxas (1871-1941), military dictator of Greece at the time of the German invasion.

Greek general discussing surrender of Greece with Germans. April 27, 1941.

the Germans poured into Greece and quickly overcame the Greek forces and the 60,000 British troops who were assisting them. The Germans occupied both Greece and Crete as the king and his government fled into exile.

The occupation was a horror which can hardly be described. The country had already been depleted by the sacrifices it had made in resisting the Italians. When the occupation stopped the vital imports of food and prohibited export from one area of Greece to another, famine was the result. It was aggravated by the Nazi policies of requisitioning anything they wanted and of taking reprisals against the Greeks for any acts of resistance. Once more Greek resistance organized in the mountains and continually harassed the Germans.

Americans, as well as the whole free world, shared a deep pride in Greek resistance and a concern for a people which the Germans seemed determined to destroy. Within two weeks of the invasion of Greece the Greek War Relief Association (GWRA) had been formed with Spyros Skouras at its head. Using the local chapters of AHEPA as an organization, GWRA reached every segment of the Greek community with its requests for help. A few months later President Roosevelt addressed these remarks to a group of Ahepans during their annual visit to the White House:

During the Hellenic war of independence more than a century ago, our young nation, prizing its own lately-won independence, expressed its ardent sympathy for the Greeks and hoped for Hellenic victory. The victory was achieved.

Today, at a far more perilous period in the history of Hellas, we intend to give full effect to our settled policy of extending all available material aid to a free people defending themselves against aggression. Such aid has been and will continue to be extended to Greece.

Whatever may be the temporary outcome of the present phase of the war...the people of Greece can count on the help and support of the government and the people of the United States.

All America responded to the plea. During its two and a half years of activity, the GWRA sent over 100 million dollars worth of food, clothing, medicine and other supplies to the citizens of Greece. Swedish vessels carried the goods and a Red Cross commission saw that the goods were distributed only to Greeks. Many thousands of Greeks were saved by these supplies at the same time that thousands of others died of starvation and diseases related to malnutrition. Because of a condition made by the Nazis, the Greeks did not know that the supplies had come from America until after the war.

Greek prisoners of war before the surrender to Germany. April 9, 1941.

When America entered the war, Greek-Americans turned their attention to the American war effort. In two great bond drives the Greek-Americans contributed over 150 million dollars. Greek families also lent their sons to the armed forces where many distinguished themselves by their heroic deeds. One of them, Christos Karaberis, won the Congressional Medal of Honor for his astonishing performance in eliminating five machine gun nests, killing eight and capturing 22 German soldiers during one action in the Italian campaign.

Because of the admiration the entire world felt for the Greek resistance and the pride they felt in their own contribution, World War II marks the beginning of a new attitude of pride among the younger Greek-Americans. They finally began to feel about their Greek heritage as their parents and grandparents hoped they might.

President Truman presents the Congressional Medal of Honor to **Christos Karaberis** for his heroism in World War II.

Distribution of Greek-Born in the U.S.*

New York	36,579
Illinois	16,660
California	14,491
Massachusetts	13,519
Ohio	8,872
Pennsylvania	8,816
Michigan	7,782
Florida	3,720
Connecticut	3,459
Indiana	3,517

*This table (1960) represents only Greek immigrants and not succeeding generations.

5. *The Contemporary Scene*

For about 40 years, from the mid–1920's to the mid–1960's, Greek immigration was limited to a quota of 308 per year. About 56,000 during these years were able to enter outside the quota: refugees after World War II, some repatriates who had been trapped by World War II, and students during the 1950's. In 1960 there were 167,000 persons of Greek birth in the United States. The quota system was the result of anti-foreign prejudice in America during the twenties, expecially prejudice against Mediterranean and Oriental peoples. In 1965 a new immigration system which did away with the quotas went into effect. This law allows a quota of 170,000 immigrants a year, 60,000 non-quota immigrants with a limit of 20,000 from any one country. Immigrants with relatives in the United States or with special skills will be given preference. It is to be expected that Greece, whose quota has been oversubscribed for many years, will take advantage of the new regulations.

In April of 1967 Greece once more faced a serious political crisis. A committee of military officers overthrew the constitutional government by force and threat of force. They claimed that they were trying to prevent a communist take-over of the government. Several thousand political leaders and politically active citizens were arrested. Among them were the Prime Minister George Papandreou and his son Andreas, a political leader who is

Andreas Papandreou is the son of the former Premier of Greece, George Papandreou. He too is an active political leader, as well as an economist who has taught at American universities.

also an economics professor. The elder Papandreou was an important figure in organizing a government which could take over after the Nazi occupation. Andreas taught in several American universities after World War II and became an American citizen. He resumed his Greek citizenship in 1964. Both Papandreous were released but Andreas left Greece soon afterward. Several purges removed other suspect citizens from the army and the universities. Other totalitarian restrictions were placed on political activity,

Melina Mercouri

Katina Paxinou, as Pilar in the film *For Whom the Bell Tolls*.

the press, and the artists of Greece. In 1968 the world famous actress Katina Paxinou, who won an Academy Award for her performance in the American film *For Whom the Bell Tolls,* quit her position in the Greek National Theatre because of the control the government placed on the repertoire of the theatre. Melina Mercouri, the film star, was declared an enemy of the state and denied her Greek citizenship because she spoke out against the junta. Other artists are in prison, exile, or living and working under government surveillance.

All of these events are of special interest and concern to the Greeks in America and once more newspapers and magazines are printing articles and letters about the political situation in Greece. America was forced to decide whether to treat the dictatorial junta as an outlaw government and refuse to give it aid, or to recognize the military leaders and hope that they will hold elections as they have promised. She recognized the new government early in 1968 after it had been in power for nine months. Perhaps the scene is now set for a new chapter in the story of Greek immigration in America.

The Greek-Americans are not numerous, but they are distinctive; their language, folkways, and religious ceremonies are unusual and interesting. Their history from the earliest times to the present is something that we share and from which we draw continuing inspiration. Far out of proportion to their numbers are the contributions made to American life by these proud people.

Scuffle following Greek Liberation Parade in New York City, 1968.

...INDEX...

ACKNOWLEDGMENTS

The illustrations are reproduced through the courtesy of: pp. 6, 11, 53, Greek National Tourist Office; p. 8, Minnesota Theatre Company; p. 10, Walker Art Center; p. 13, Louvre, Paris, Photo Alinari; p. 15, Museo Capitolino, Rome, Photo Alinari; p. 18, Independent Picture Service; p. 21, British Columbia Government; pp. 22 (left and right), 23, 24, Dr. Carita Doggett Corse; p. 26, U. S. Department of Interior, National Park Service; p. 29 (left), *Dictionary of American Portraits*, Dover Publications, Inc.; p. 29 (right), Bureau of Naval Personnel, National Archives; p. 30, State Historical Society of Wisconsin; p. 31 (left and right), Perkins School for the Blind; pp. 35, 38, *Greek Immigration to the United States*, Yale University Press; pp. 36, 43, 45, 46, 56, Theodore Koutras; p. 40, Nebraska State Historical Society; p. 48, Annunciation Church; p. 49 (left and right), Greek Orthodox Archdiocese of North and South America; p. 50, Panhellenic University; p. 52 (left), *Atlantis*; p. 52 (right), Dr. Theodore Saloutas, *The Greeks in the United States*, Harvard University Press; p. 58 (top, left and right), Office of the Congressmen; p. 58 (bottom), Nixon-Agnew Campaign Committee; p. 59 (left), 20th Century Fox Film Corporation; p. 59 (right), Standard Oil Company; p. 61 (top), Metropolitan Opera Archives; p. 61 (bottom), Minneapolis Symphony Orchestra; p. 62 (left), Elia Kazan; p. 62 (right), CBS News; p. 63 (left), Cincinnati Reds, Inc.; p. 63 (right), Detroit Lions; p. 64, Cornell University Medical College, Barrett Gallagher Photo; p. 65, Washington University, Herb Weitman Photo; p. 66, Herb Comess Photo; p. 68, John Vassos; p. 68, U. S. Information Agency, National Archives; pp. 69, 70, World War II Collection, National Archives; p. 71, U. S. Army Photograph, Pentagon; p. 73, Minneapolis *Tribune*; p. 74, United Artists Corporation; p. 75, MCA, Inc.; p. 76, New York *Tribune*.

ABOUT THE AUTHOR...

JAYNE CLARK JONES is a graduate of the University of Minnesota. A life-long philhellene, her childhood interest in classical mythology grew until it included an undergraduate minor in classical Greek and graduate study in ancient history and classical Greek literature. This interest has since expanded to include informal study of modern Greek language, history, and literature. Mrs. Jones's enthusiasms are shared, in depth, by her husband Tom Jones, Professor of Ancient History at the University of Minnesota. The long and lively history of Greek-American relations and the current American concern about Greek political affairs reenforce Mrs. Jones's feeling that anytime is a good time to be interested in Greece. Dr. and Mrs. Jones live with their five children in Minneapolis.

The IN AMERICA *Series*

The CZECHS *and* SLOVAKS *in America*
The DUTCH *in America*
The EAST INDIANS *and* PAKISTANIS *in America*
The ENGLISH *in America*
The FRENCH *in America*
The GERMANS *in America*
The GREEKS *in America*
The HUNGARIANS *in America*
The IRISH *in America*
The ITALIANS *in America*
The JAPANESE *in America*
The JEWS *in America*
The NEGRO *in America*
The NORWEGIANS *in America*
The POLES *in America*
The SCOTS *and* SCOTCH-IRISH *in America*
The SWEDES *in America*
The FREEDOM OF THE PRESS *in America*
The FREEDOM OF RELIGION *in America*
The FREEDOM OF SPEECH *in America*

We specialize in publishing quality books for
young people. For a complete list please write:

LERNER PUBLICATIONS COMPANY
241 First Avenue North, Minneapolis, Minnesota 55401